ABC 123

For Ages 3+

Writing Workbook

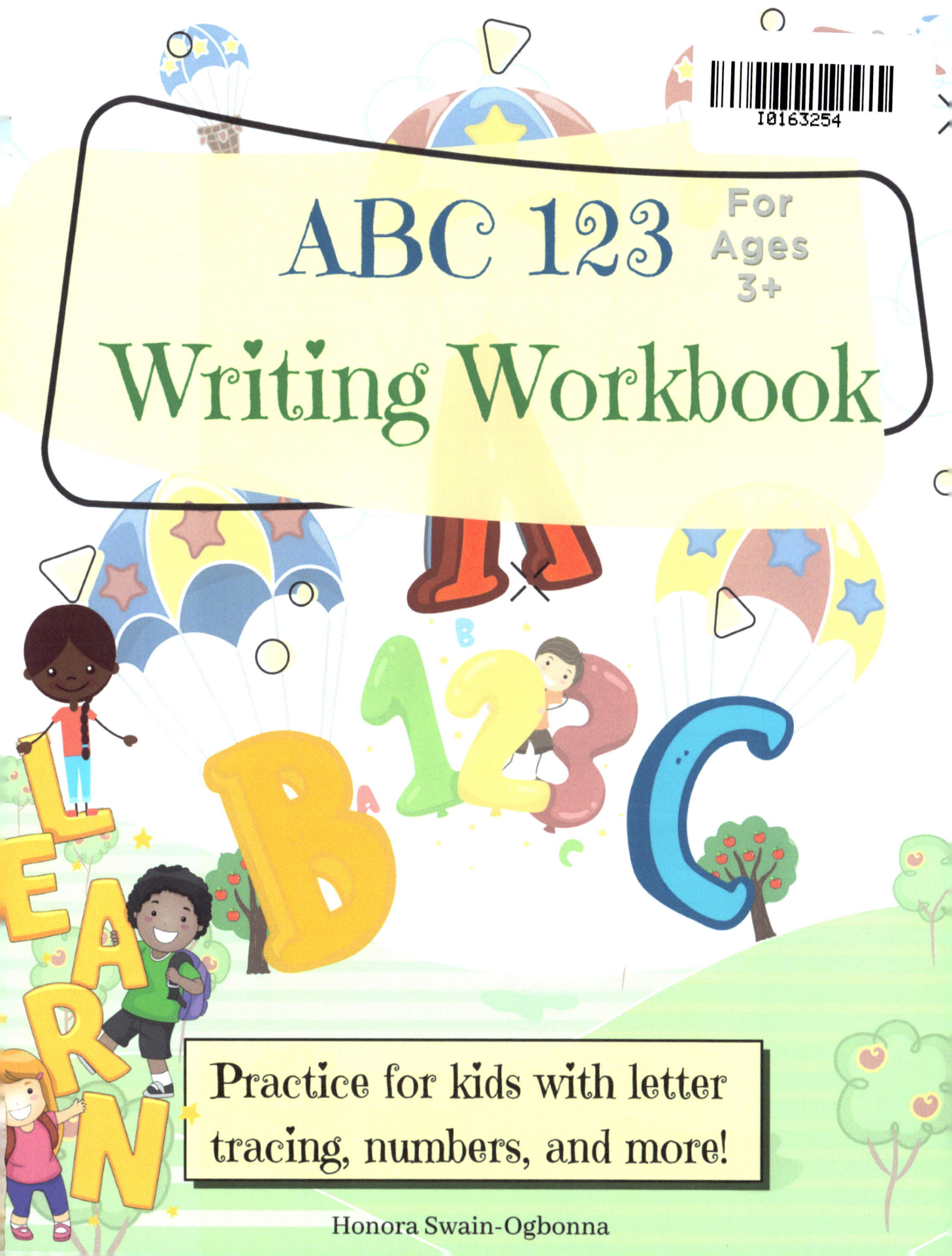

Practice for kids with letter tracing, numbers, and more!

Honora Swain-Ogbonna

Note to Parents

This book is designed to help children develop and grow their writing skills.

In this book, your child will able to:

1. Strengthen fine motor skills
2. Practice staying on dotted lines
3. Learn how to trace letters from A to Z
4. Learn how to trace numbers from zero to ten.

I hope that your child enjoys this book and that it is helpful in teaching them writing skills.

Have fun writing!

Directions

This book will start by having your child trace letters then numbers. Your child will get practice tracing both lower and upper case letters and numbers from zero to 10.

It is recommended that you allow your child to practice their writing by following the book in page order.

It is also strongly encouraged that you allow your child to practice writing by using a crayon or pencil that is short and fat. Also ensure that your child has a firm grip on their writing tool.

This Book
Belongs to:

_____

- -

_____

Letter A

Let's learn and trace the letter Aa. Then complete the coloring activity.

A is for  apple

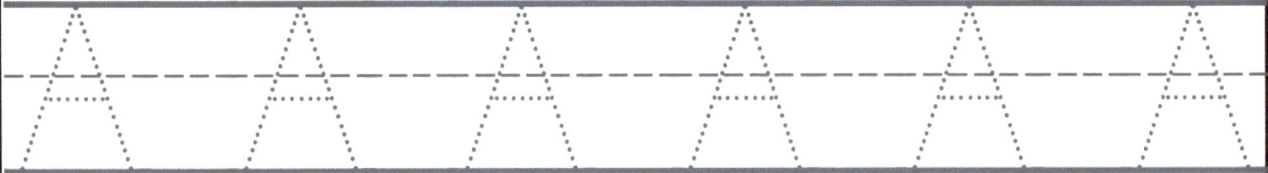

Letter B

Let's learn and trace the letter Bb. Then complete the coloring activity.

B is for

butterfly

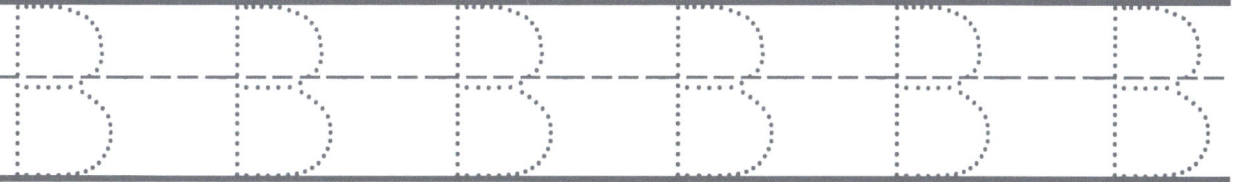

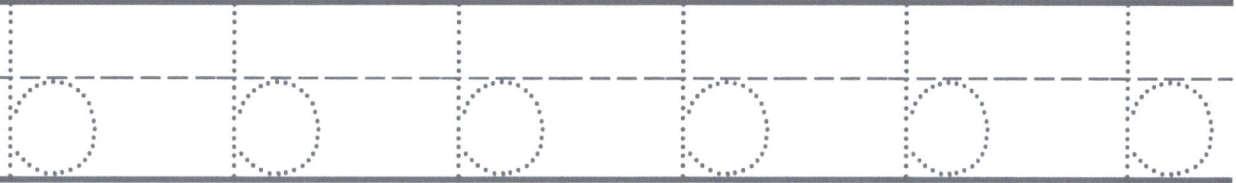

Bb

Letter C

Let's learn and trace the letter Cc. Then complete the coloring activity.

C

is for

cat

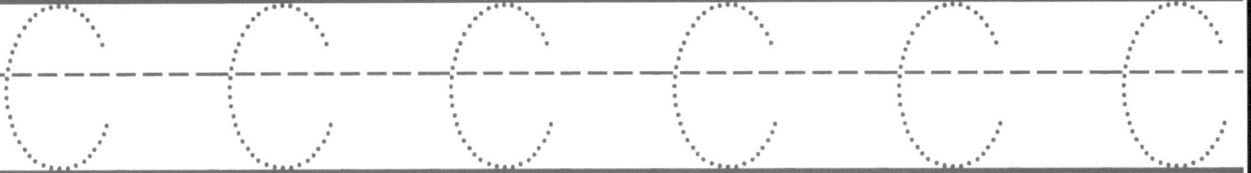

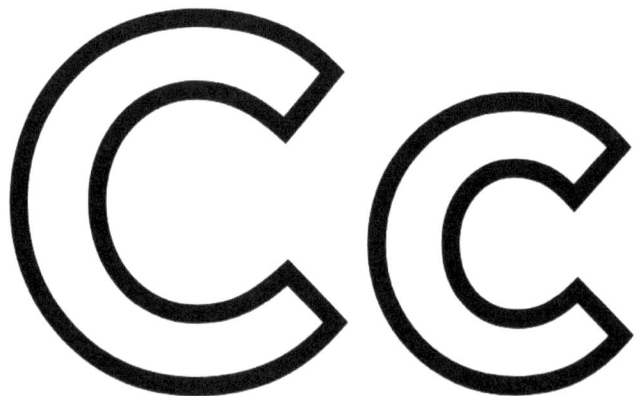

Letter D

Let's learn and trace the letter Dd. Then complete the coloring activity.

D is for

duck

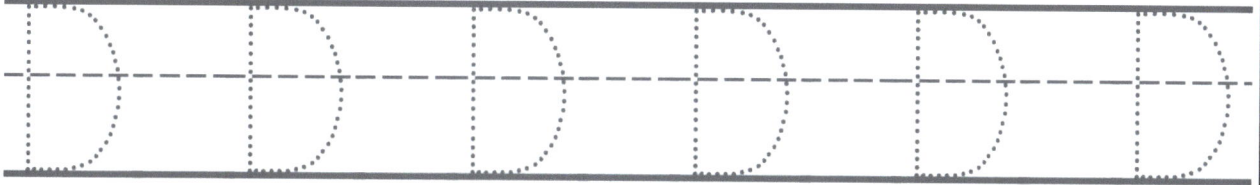

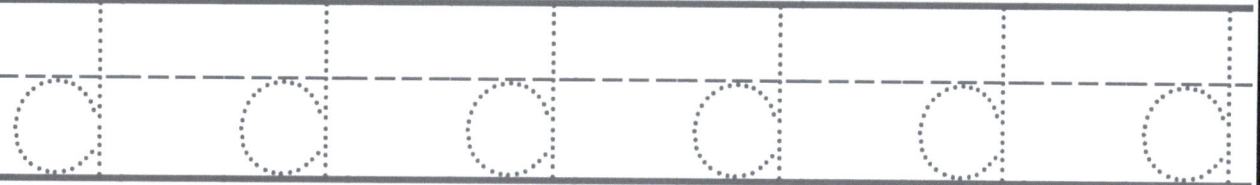

Dd

Let's learn and trace the letter Ee. Then complete the coloring activity.

E

is for

elephant

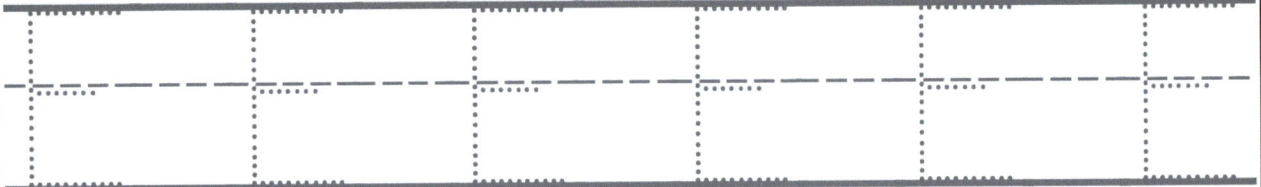

Ee

Let's learn and trace the letter Ff. Then complete the coloring activity.

F

is for

fish

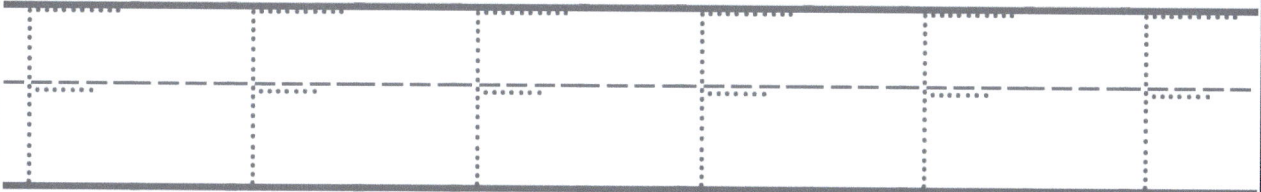

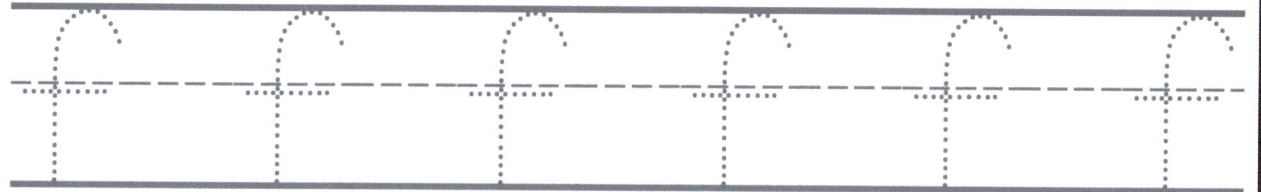

Ff

Letter G

Let's learn and trace the letter Gg. Then complete the coloring activity.

G

is for

grapes

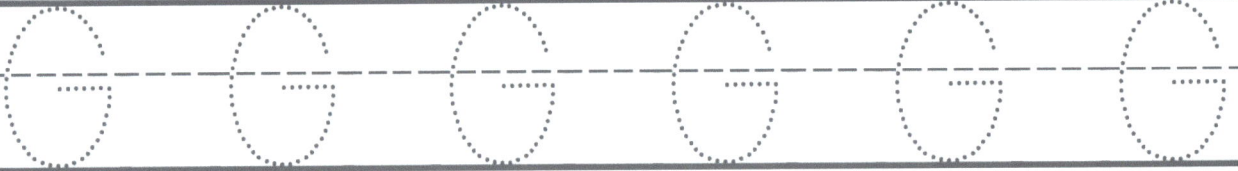

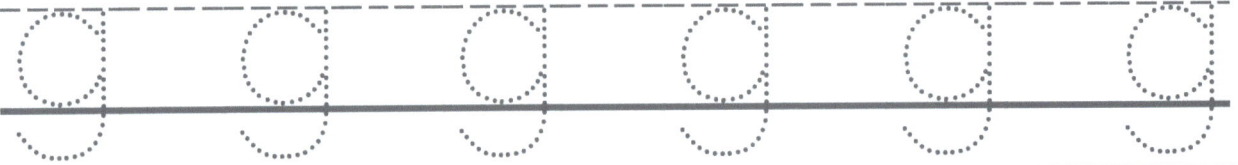

Letter H

Let's learn and trace the letter Hh. Then complete the coloring activity.

H

is for

hat

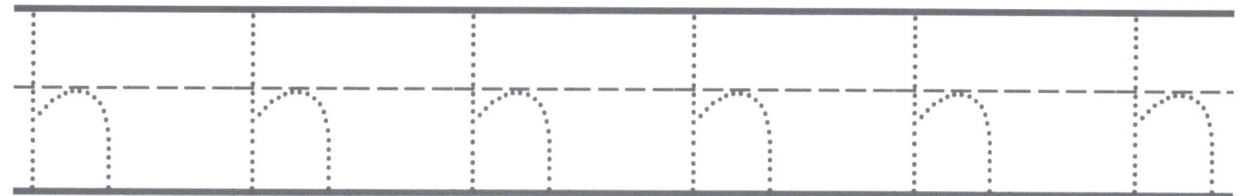

Hh

Letter I

Let's learn and trace the letter Ii. Then complete the coloring activity.

 is for  igloo

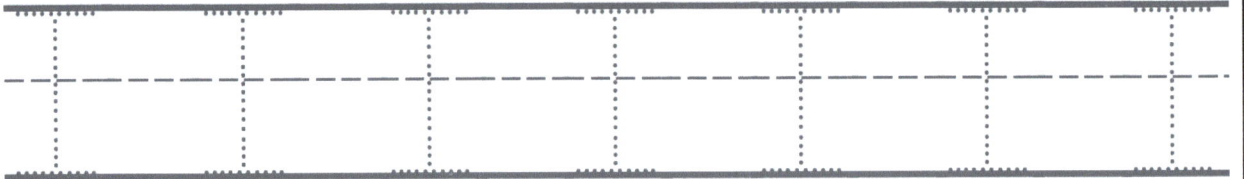

Let's learn and trace the letter Jj. Then complete the coloring activity.

J

is for

jelly

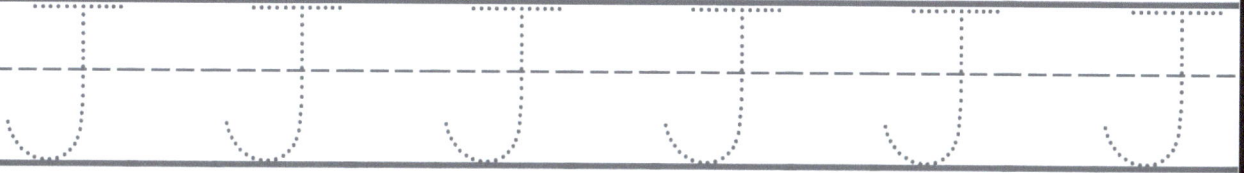

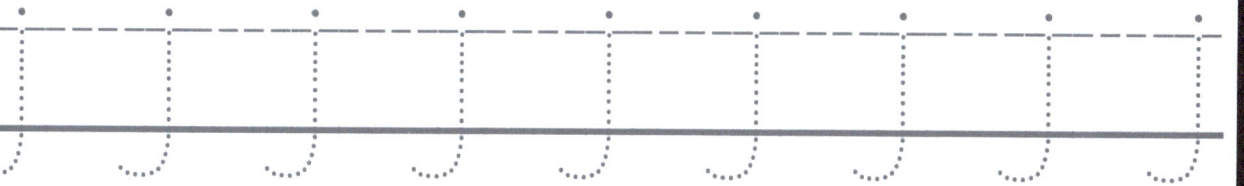

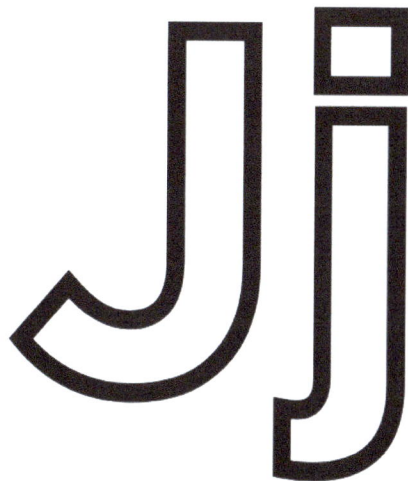

Let's learn and trace the letter Kk. Then complete the coloring activity.

K

is for

kangaroo

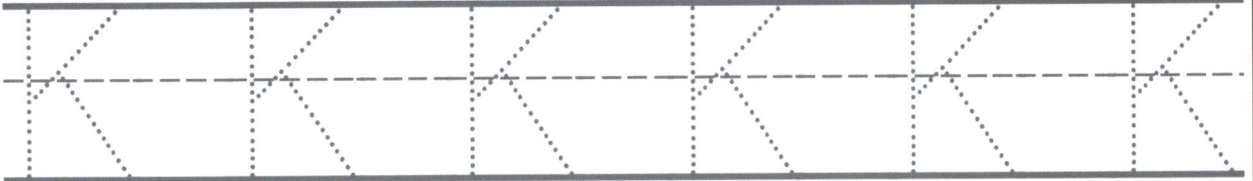

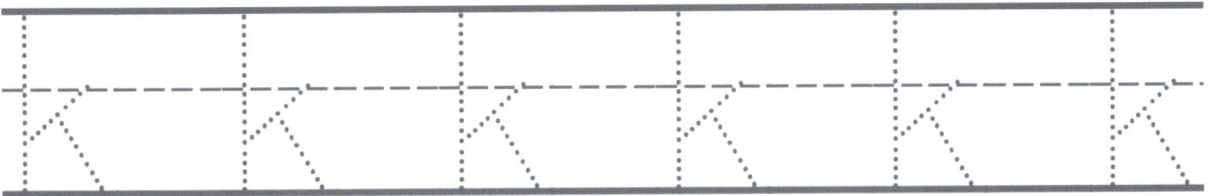

Kk

Letter L

Let's learn and trace the letter Ll. Then complete the coloring activity.

L **is for**  **lion**

Let's learn and trace the letter Mm. Then complete the coloring activity.

M

is for

moon

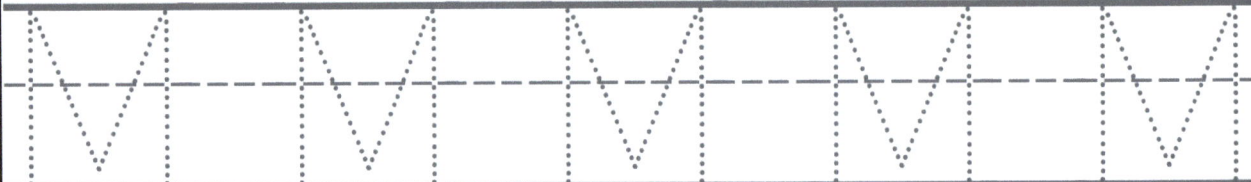

Let's learn and trace the letter Nn. Then complete the coloring activity.

N is for

nest

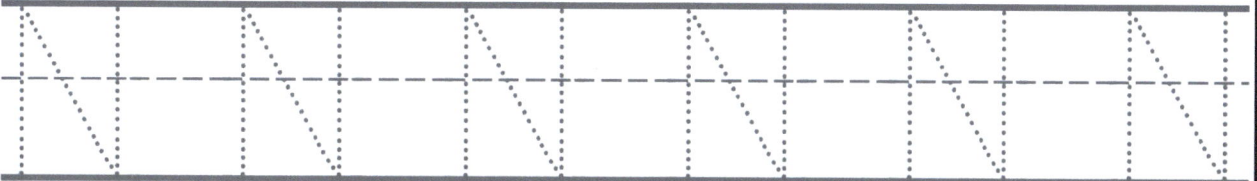

Letter O

Let's learn and trace the letter Oo. Then complete the coloring activity.

 **is for**

octopus

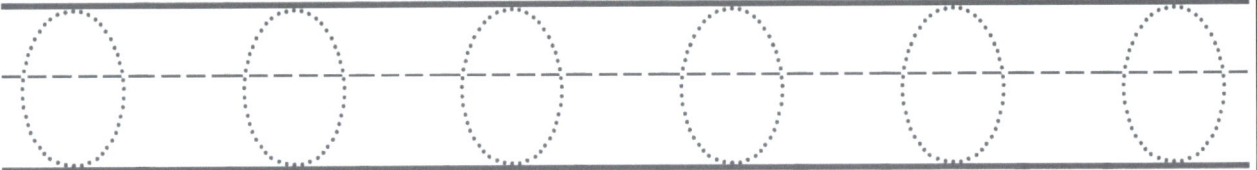

 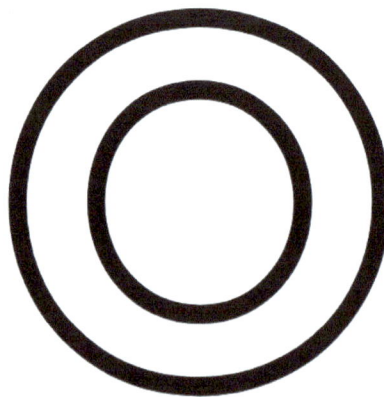 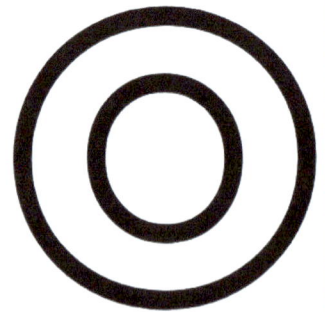

Let's learn and trace the letter Pp. Then complete the coloring activity.

P

is for

parrot

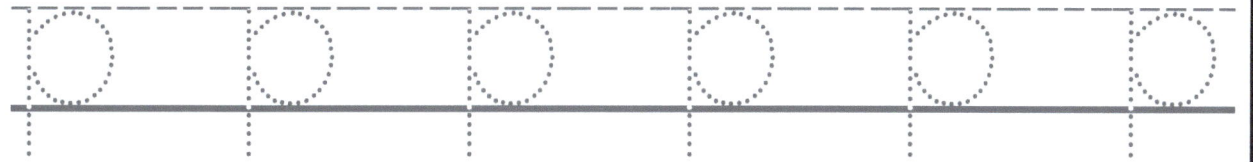

Pp

Letter Q

Let's learn and trace the letter Qq. Then complete the coloring activity.

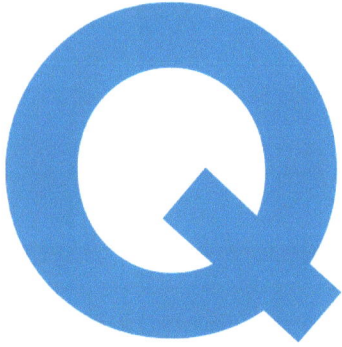 **is for**

queen

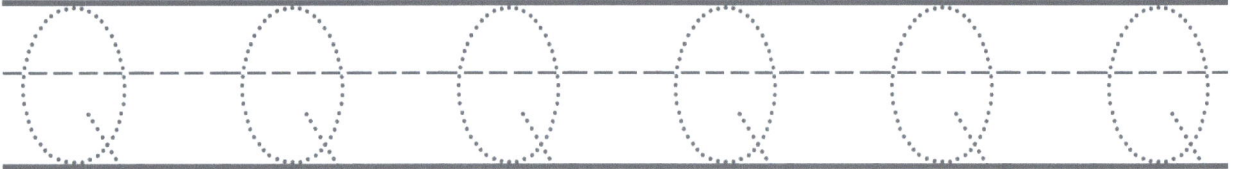

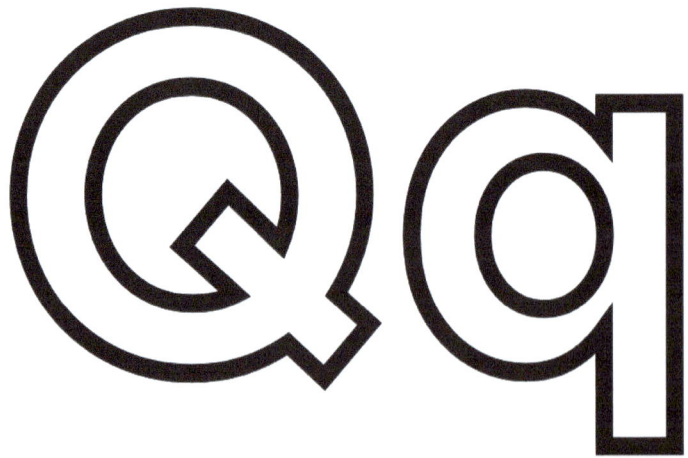

Letter R

Let's learn and trace the letter Rr. Then complete the coloring activity.

R is for

rose

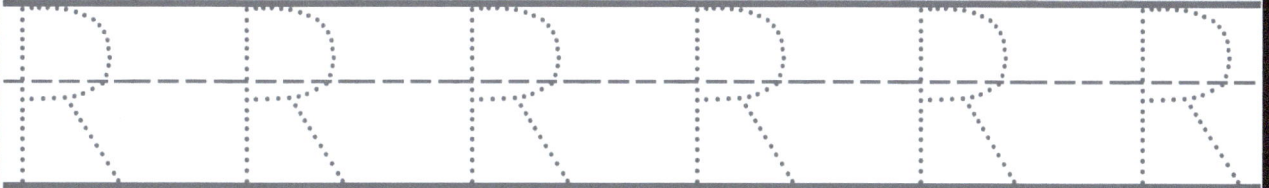

Rr

Letter S

Let's learn and trace the letter Ss. Then complete the coloring activity.

S **is for**  **star**

Letter T

Let's learn and trace the letter Tt. Then complete the coloring activity.

T

T **is for**  **tiger**

Tt

Let's learn and trace the letter Uu. Then complete the coloring activity.

U

is for

unicorn

Uu

Let's learn and trace the letter Vv. Then complete the coloring activity.

V

is for

violin

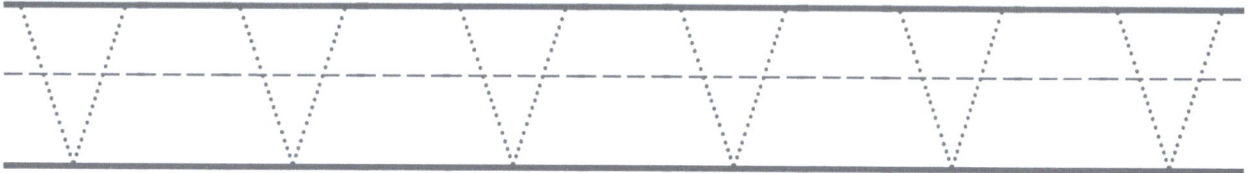

Vv

Letter W

Let's learn and trace the letter Ww. Then complete the coloring activity.

W is for

window

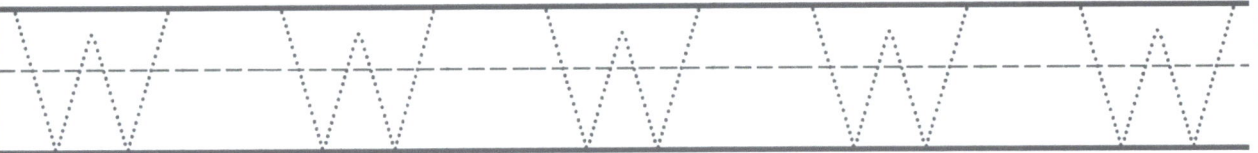

Letter X

Let's learn and trace the letter Xx. Then complete the coloring activity.

X

is for
xylophone

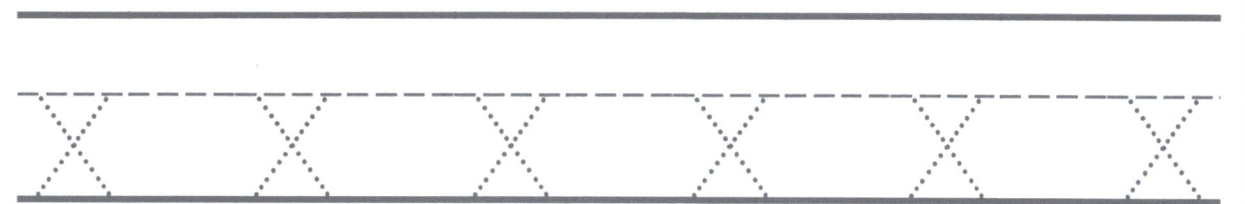

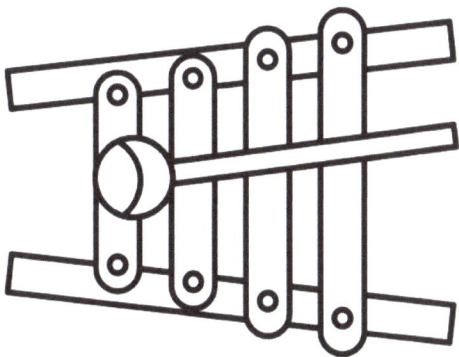
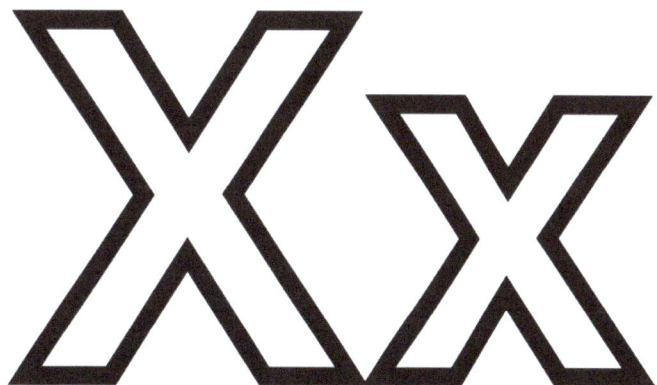

Letter Y

Let's learn and trace the letter Yy. Then complete the coloring activity.

Y is for

yak

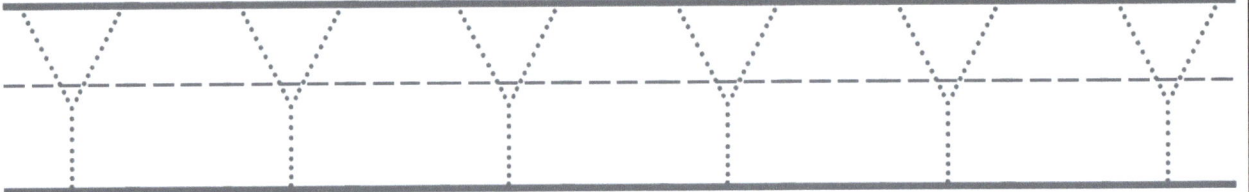

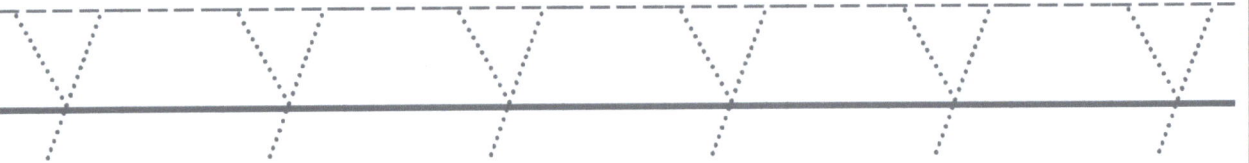

Letter Z

Let's learn and trace the letter Zz. Then complete the coloring activity.

Z

is for

zipper

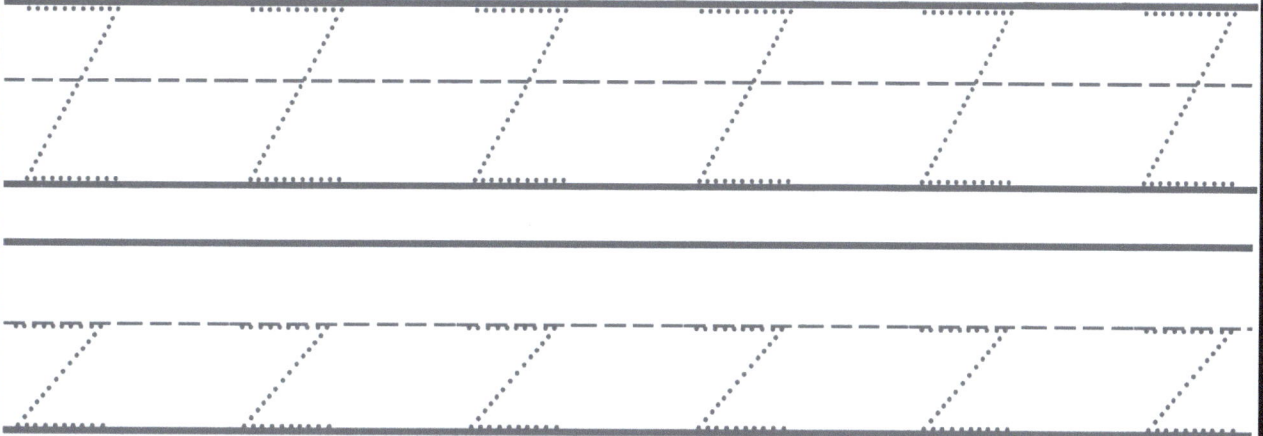

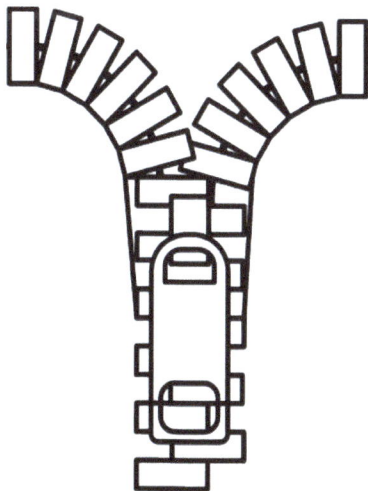

Aa-Zz

Now trace all the capital and small letters

A B C D E F G H I J

K L M N O P Q R S

T U V W X Y Z

a b c d e f g h i j

k l m n o p q r s t

u v w x y z

Practice writing your name here.

Uppercase

Lowercase

One 1

Let's count, trace, and write the number one.

1

Two 2

Let's count, trace, and write the number two.

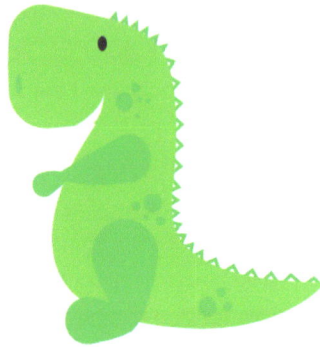

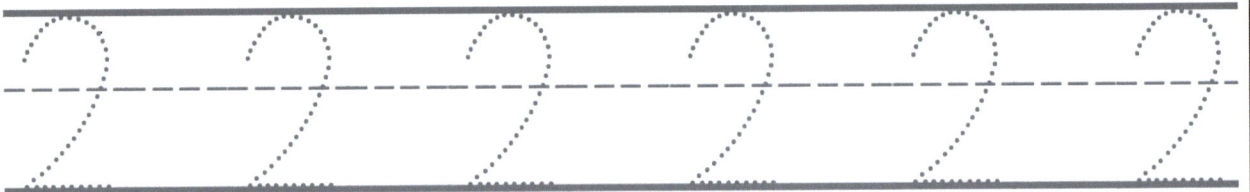

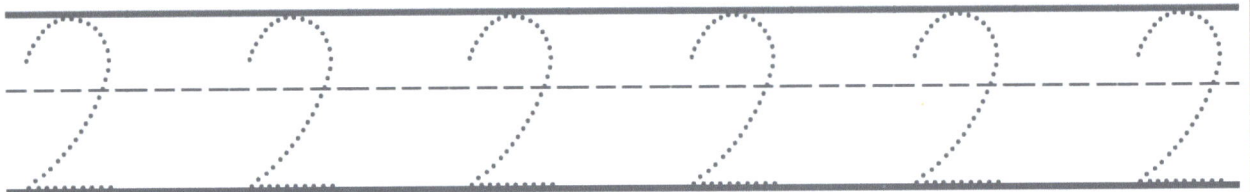

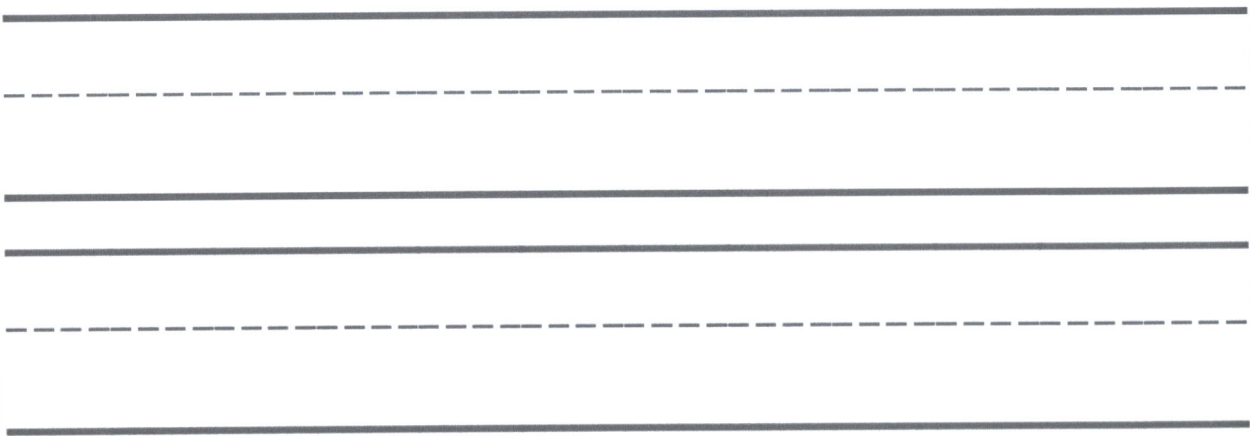

2

2 2 2 2 2

2 2 2 2 2

2 2 2 2 2

Three 3

Let's count, trace, and write the number three.

3

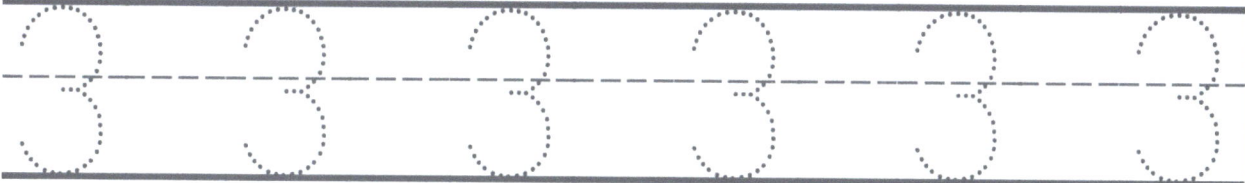

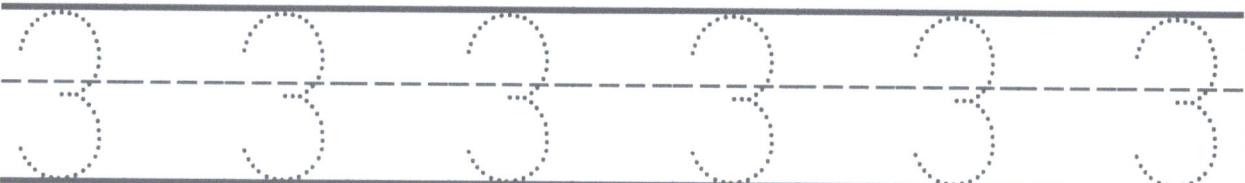

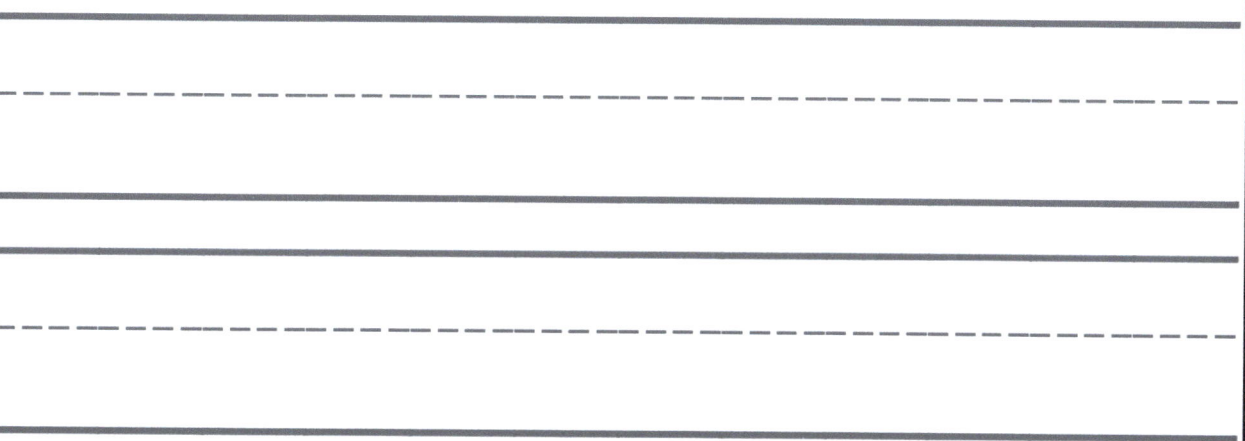

Four 4

Let's count, trace, and write the number four.

4

Five 5

Let's count, trace, and write the number five.

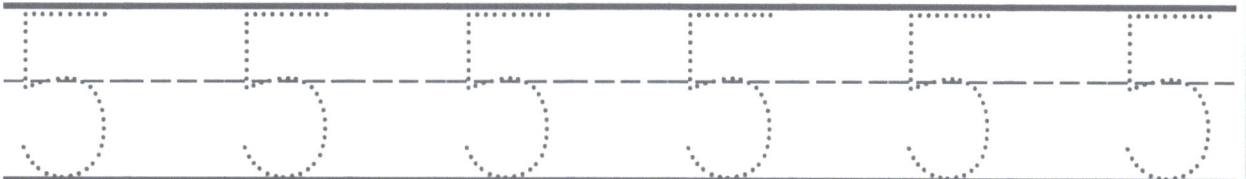

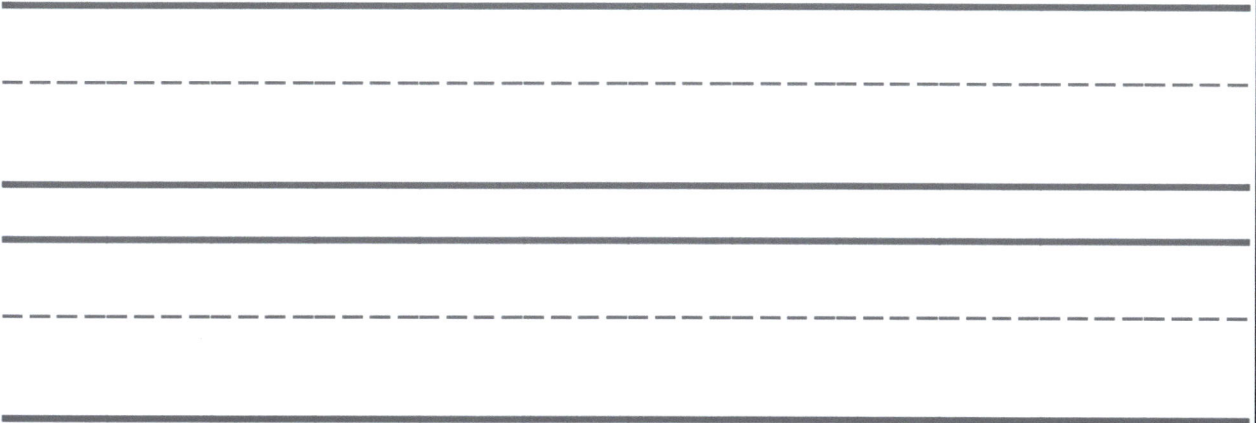

Six 6

Let's count, trace, and write the number six.

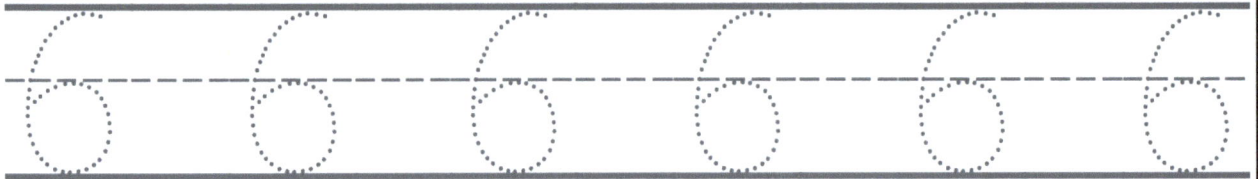

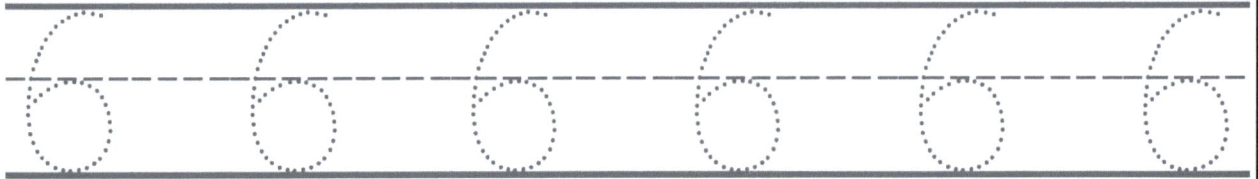

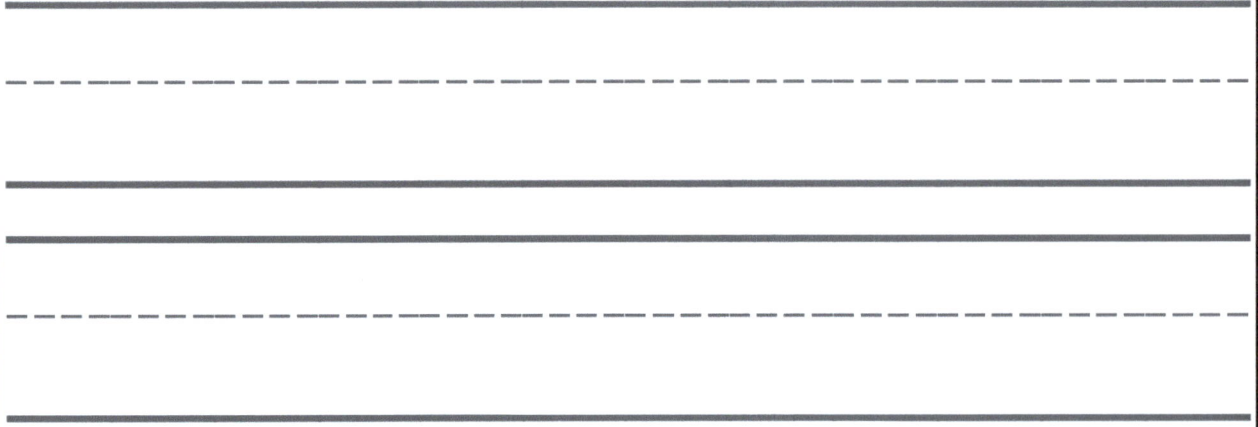

6

Seven 7

Let's count, trace, and write the number seven.

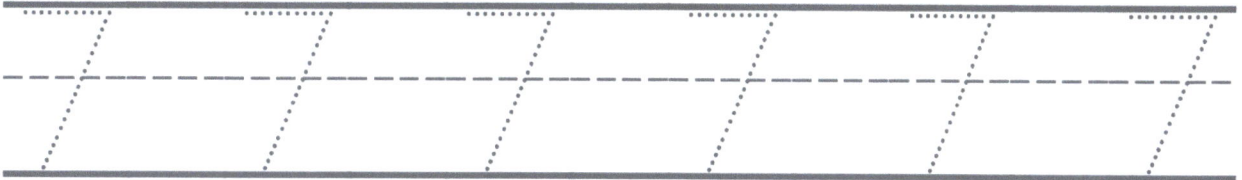

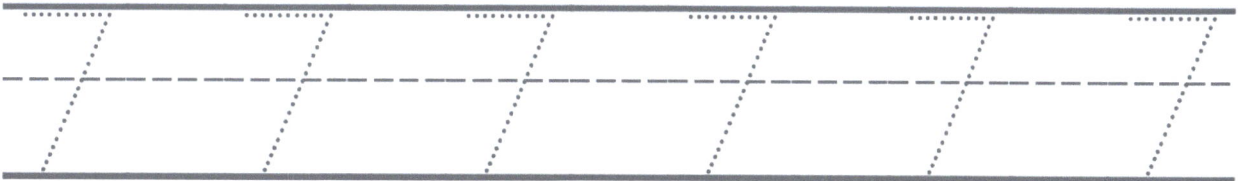

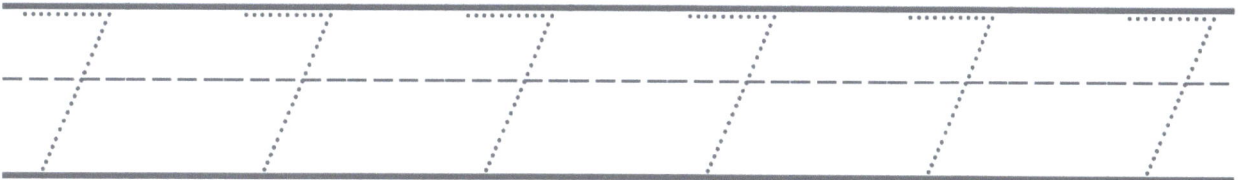

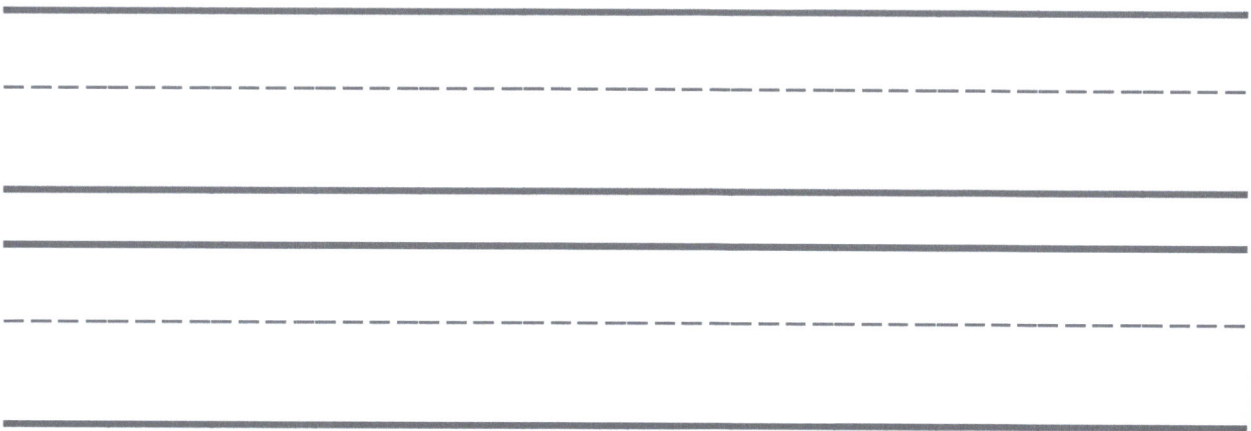

Eight 8

Let's count, trace, and write the number eight.

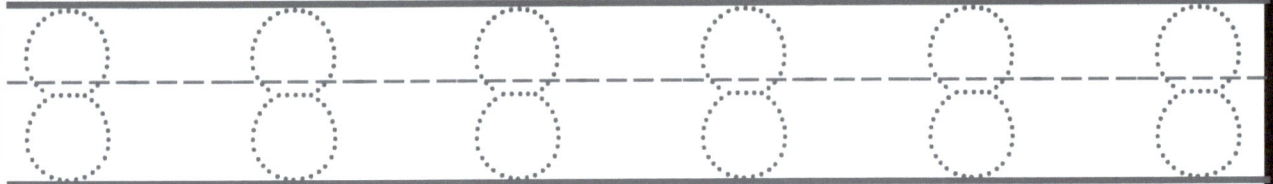

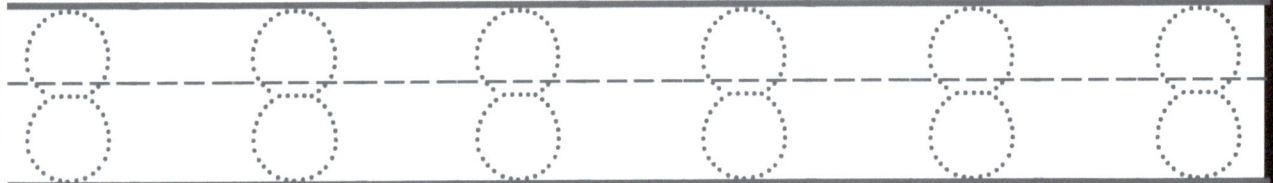

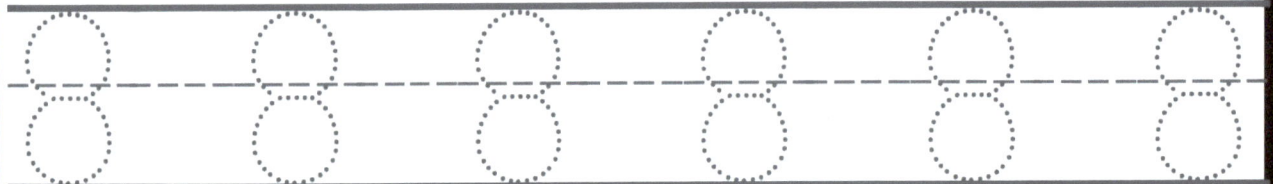

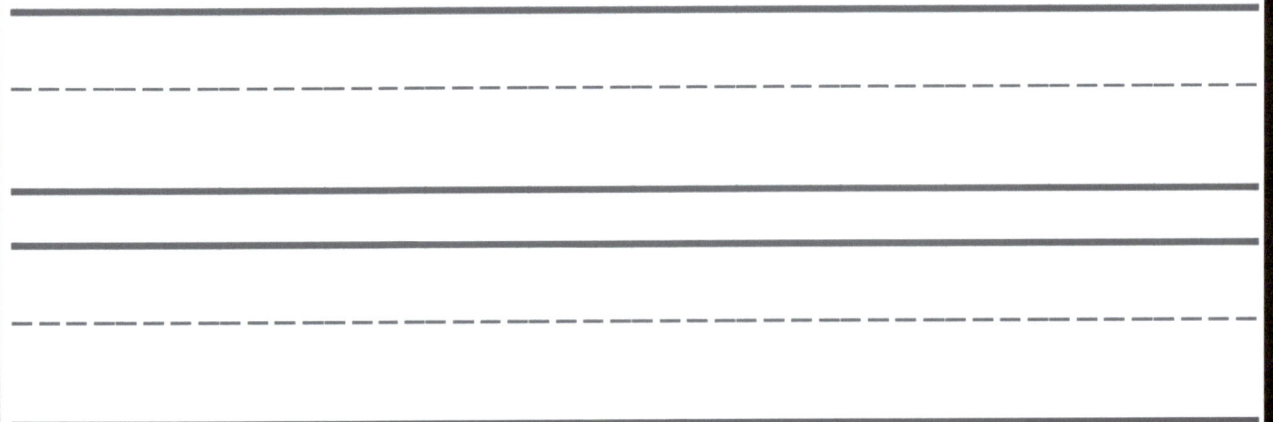

8

Nine 9

Let's count, trace, and write the number nine.

Ten 10

Let's count, trace, and write the number ten.

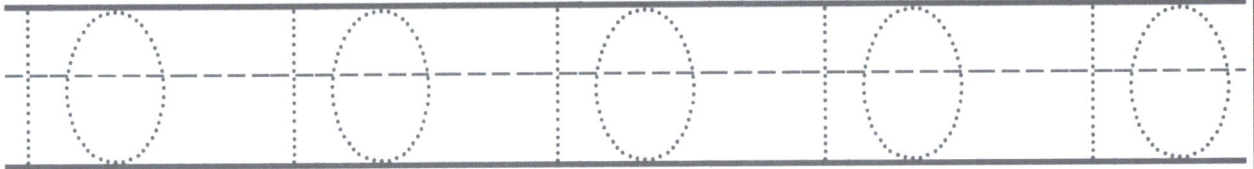

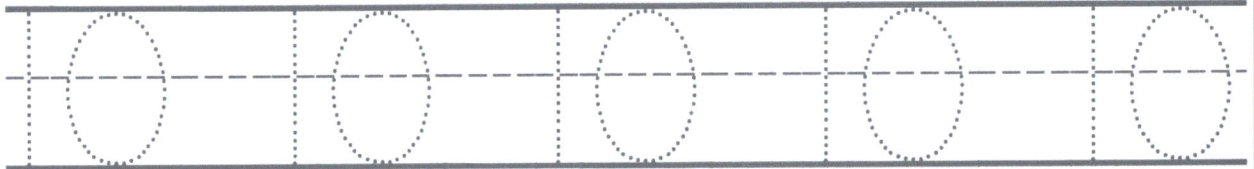

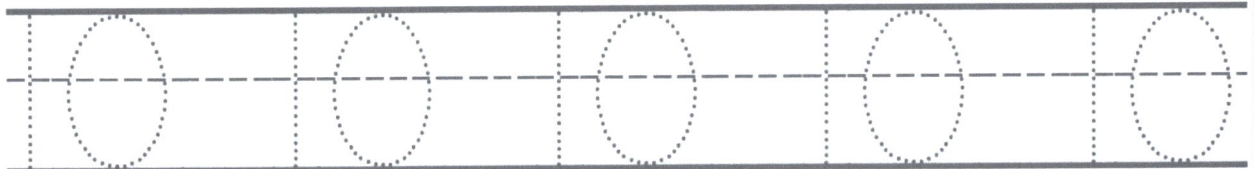

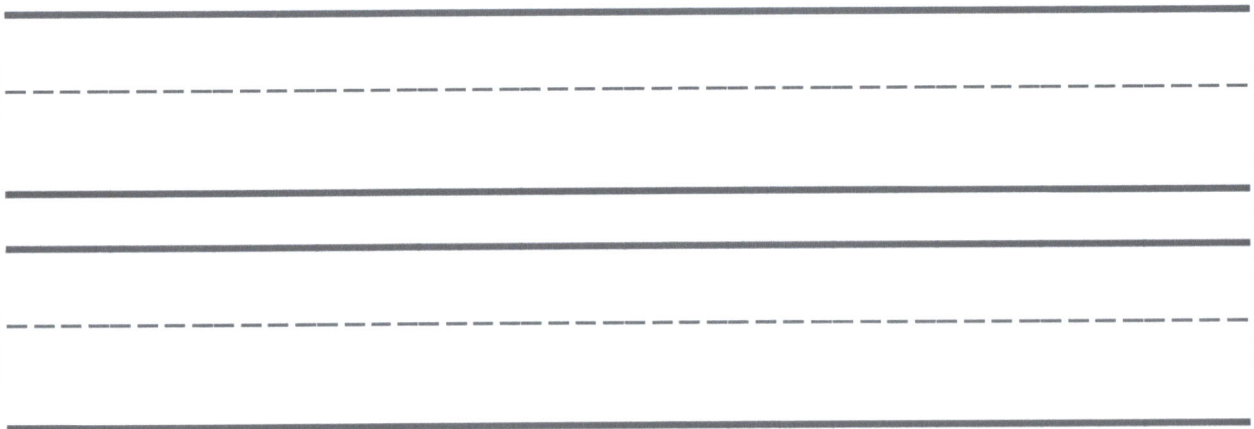

One-Ten

Now trace and write all the numbers from 1-10. Then color and count the objects below.

1 2 3 4 5 6 7 8 9 10
1 2 3 4 5 6 7 8 9 10
1 2 3 4 5 6 7 8 9 10

CERTIFICATE OF ACHIEVEMENT

This certificate is presented to

for learning how to write!

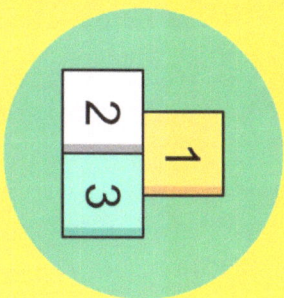

"About the Author"

Honora Swain-Ogbonna is a public health professional and writer. Her public health career has focused on the physical and mental well-being of youth. Her experience in public health and as a mother has made helping children and youth a personal mission. She hopes that this book will aid in improving the writing skills of children which can also result in the enhancement of childhood literacy.